BRITISH MUSEUM

FUN BOOK

ANCIENT
EGYPT

Sandy Ransford
Illustrated by David Farris

BRITISH MUSEUM 📖 PRESS

CONTENTS

Checklist

If you don't know much about ancient Egypt, some of the words and names in this book may seem strange to you. The lists below explain who or what they are. They may help you to solve some of the puzzles.

PHARAOHS, KINGS AND QUEENS

Chephren
King

Cleopatra
Queen, ruled jointly with her brother Ptolemy XII

Djoser
King, who built the Step Pyramid at Saqqara

Hatshepsut
Queen, who built a famous temple at Deir el-Bahri

Itakayt
Princess, built a pyramid

Khafre
King, built a pyramid at Giza

Khephren
King

Khufu
King (also known as Cheops) who built the Great Pyramid at Giza

Menkaura
King who built the third pyramid at Giza

Neferu
Queen, built a pyramid

Ramses
The name of several kings

Ramses II
Built temples at Abu Simbel and Thebes

Senwosret
King, built a pyramid

Sneferu
King, built the 'Bent' Pyramid at Maidum

Thutmose
The name of four kings

Tutankhamun
Boy king who died at 18. He became famous because of the treasure found in his tomb

GODS

Anubis
God who led the dead to judgement. He has a jackal's head

Bast (or Bastet)
Goddess. She is shown as a cat or with a cat's head

Horus
God of the sky. He has the head of a falcon

Isis
Goddess, wife of Osiris and mother of Horus. She is sometimes shown with cow's horns

Khnum
Ram-headed god

Osiris
God of the underworld, often shown as a mummy

OTHERS

Abu Simbel
Temple built by King Ramses II. It has four massive statues of him. It was moved and rebuilt this century during the building of the Aswan dam

Dynasty
A succession of kings or queens of the same family

Imhotep
Chief architect of King Djoser, responsible for building the king's pyramid

Natron
A cleansing substance used in mummification

Papyrus
A tall plant whose stems were used for making paper

Sarcophagus
A stone coffin

KNOCK, KNOCK.
WHO'S THERE?
THEBES.
THEBES WHO?
THEBES HAB STOLEN
ALL OUR GOLD.

INTRODUCTION

Ancient Egypt makes us think of the pyramids, and marvel at how those vast structures were built without the benefit of modern engineering. We think of the exquisite jewellery and artefacts found in the tombs, of the huge statues and temples, and the strange animal-headed gods. Most of all, we enjoy the creepy feelings all those mummified bodies wrapped in bandages send shivering through us.

The history of ancient Egypt spans approximately 3,500 years, from the pre-dynastic period around 3,000 BC to the Graeco-Roman period around AD 500. This book is a collection of puzzles based on the people, places and events of those times. Baffling brainteasers, crosswords, word-searches, quizzes and picture puzzles will challenge your wits; and there are games to play and a good number of ancient jokes scattered about to make you laugh. I hope you find it lots of fun, and that it will spur you on to find out even more about this fascinating subject.

HOW DO YOU SHOCK A MUSEUM CURATOR?

WALK UP TO HIM AND ASK 'WHAT'S NEW?'

MONUMENTAL

There were over 80 pyramids in ancient Egypt, though only a few are well-known today. Listed below are 19 names of people and places connected with them, and you can find them all in the grid on the opposite page. The words may run across, up, down or diagonally, either forwards or backwards, but they are all in straight lines. Letters may be used more than once, though not all the letters are necessarily used.

People
CHEPHREN
DJOSER
IMHOTEP
ITAKAYT
KHAFRE
KHUFU
MENKAURA
NEFERU
SENWOSRET
SNEFERU

Places
ASWAN
DAHSHUR
GIZA
LISHT
MAIDUM
MEMPHIS
NILE
SAQQARA
TURA

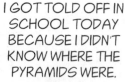

I GOT TOLD OFF IN SCHOOL TODAY BECAUSE I DIDN'T KNOW WHERE THE PYRAMIDS WERE.

YOU SHOULD REMEMBER WHERE YOU PUT YOUR THINGS.

BUILDING COSTS

1   The Step Pyramid at Saqqara, built around 2,650 BC, is the oldest large stone building in the world. Along with other buildings it was enclosed by a wall 500 m (547 yds) long and 300 m (328 yds) wide.
    What was the total area enclosed?

2   King Khufu's Great Pyramid is believed to have contained 2,300,000 blocks of stone. Most of it was quarried close by, but the fine white limestone which covered the surface came from Tura, and the heavy granite which lined the chambers and passages inside came from Aswan.
    If half the stone used was local, a quarter was white limestone, and a quarter was heavy granite, how many white limestone and heavy granite blocks were used?

3   Before around 664 BC workers on the pyramids were paid monthly in wheat and barley measured in khars. One khar equalled 77 litres.
    If a foreman received 5.5 khars of wheat and 2 khars of barley per month; a workman 4 khars of wheat and 1.5 khars of barley; and a young apprentice 1.5 khars of wheat and 0.5 khars of barley, what would the monthly wages bill be on a site employing one foreman, ten workmen and six apprentices?

BIRDS OF A FEATHER

These four pictures show a bird called the sacred ibis. Although they all look the same, only two of the pictures are exactly alike. Which two are they?

READING AND WRITING

The Ancient Egyptians used little pictures, or hieroglyphs, to write down the sounds of their language. The symbols below represent the name Cleopatra, an Egyptian queen, though it is spelt KLIOPATRA in Greek style.

Using these symbols, can you work out what the words on the next page mean?

⬭ = K   ▦ = P

🦁 = L   🦅 = A

🔪 = I   ✋ = T

🪢 = O   ⬮ = R

11

IT'S THE BEST!

Hidden in each of the sentences below is a word connected with ancient Egypt. It could be the name of a place, a king, a god or a thing. For example, the word Thebes can be read in the heading, like this:
It's **the Bes**t! Can you spot them all?

1 When they climbed up the cliff, Anni led the way.

2 Did Freddie know he was wanted?

3 'Why didn't you catch a bus?' I.M. bellowed.

4 Were those rams Estelle saw in the field?

5 'Give the lame M.P. his walking-stick, Harold!'

6 'Sis, is Jennie coming round today?'

7 Who led Bob astray?

8 'Did you send an S.O.S., Iris?'

9 Angela sang in the chorus.

10 'Did anyone give Mum my packed lunch?'

Can you find the correct route through this maze of passages inside the pyramid to the pharaoh's tomb?

QUICK QUIZ

How much do you know about ancient Egypt? Find out with this quiz. Each question has three alternative answers, but only one is correct.

1 The Great Pyramid of Khufu is at:
a) Thebes b) Luxor c) Giza

2 A 'mummy' is:
a) a painted model of a human figure put in a tomb
b) a body with its organs removed, packed with linen and spices and bound with bandages
c) a coffin in which a person's body was put after death

3 King Tutankhamun died when he was:
a) 18 b) 28 c) 38

4 The Sphinx has:
a) the head of a man and the body of a lion
b) the head of a lion and the body of a man
c) the head of a man and the body of a hippopotamus

5 The ancient Egyptians used papyrus for writing on. It was prepared from:
a) the skin of a sheep
b) the bark of a palm tree
c) the stem of a reed

6 Kohl was:
a) a spice used in embalming bodies
b) a kind of make-up used to paint lines round the eyes
c) a fuel used in cooking food

7 The first pyramids were built:
a) around 2,500 BC
b) around 5,000 BC
c) around 500 BC

8 A pharaoh was:
a) a holy man
b) an Egyptian god
c) a king of Egypt

9 Floods from the Nile provided the ancient Egyptians with fertile land in which to grow food. This flooding occurred:
a) every year
b) every two years
c) every five years

10 The picture symbols the ancient Egyptians used when writing are called:
a) Coptic
b) cartouches
c) hieroglyphs

IN THE HOUSE

These six small pictures show some of the things you'd have seen around the house if you'd lived in ancient Egypt. One object appears more often than the others. Which is it?

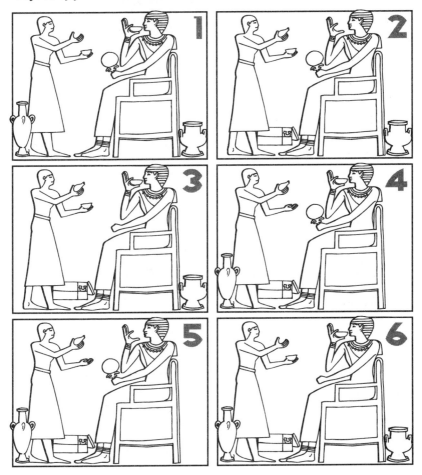

CRACK THE CROSSWORD

Solve the picture and word clues and fill in the answers in the grid. The numbers in brackets show the number of letters in each answer.

Across

1 *(6)*

4 Get up from a chair *(5)*

7 Battle at which Cleopatra was defeated in 31 BC *(6)*

9 Part of a house *(4)*

11 *(4)*

13 Building component *(5)*

17 The opposite of 'in' *(3)*

18 Donkey *(3)*

19 Bird of prey, like the god Horus *(6)*

21 The opposite of 'fat' *(4)*

23 Opposite of 'earlier' *(5)*

25 *(3)*

27 *(7)*

28 One-twelfth of the Egyptian year *(5)*

29 Egyptian river *(4)*

30 Monarch *(4)*

Down

1 *(6)*

2 The sun god *(2)*

3 *(5)*

4 19th-dynasty pharaoh, the father of Ramses II *(4)*

5 The way into a tomb *(4)*

6 Not dark *(3)*

8  *(4)*

10 Kind of tree *(3)*

12 See 14 Down

14 and 12 Inscribed rock which provided archaeologists with a key to the ancient Egyptian language *(7, 5)*

15 Box in which dead body is put for burial *(6)*

16 Another word for 19 Across *(4)*

20 *(6)*

22 Woman when she marries *(5)*

24  *(6)*

25 The name of 11 19th- and 20th-dynasty pharaohs *(6)*

26 *(6)*

17

EGYPTIAN LOUTS

Each of the odd-looking words and phrases listed below can be rearranged to make another word connected with ancient Egypt. For example, the letters of 'louts' make the word 'lotus', a kind of plant which grew in Egypt. Can you work out what the others are?

1 **RAP, HO HA.**

2 **I BLAB MUSE.**

3 **PESTS RISE.**

4 **PALE RAT CO.**

5 **TOPE HIM.**

6 **PUSH THAT S.E.**

7 **SYRUP, PA?**

8 **IN A BUS.**

HOW MANY DIFFERENCES...

... can you spot between these two pictures of Tutankhamun's beautiful gold mask?

WHAT DO EGYPTIAN MUMMIES PAINT ON THE ENDS OF THEIR FINGERS?

NILE VARNISH!

PLAY SCARAB

You will need
1 die and shaker
paper and pencil for each player

Two to six players can take part in this special ancient
Egyptian version of the old favourite game, Beetle. The
object of the game is to draw a scarab (a kind of beetle
sacred to the Egyptians), but you have to throw the
correct value on the die before you can draw each part.
Players take it in turns to throw the die.

The values are:
1 for the head
2 for the chest
3 for the left side of the body
4 for the right side of the body
5 for the feelers
6 for each leg

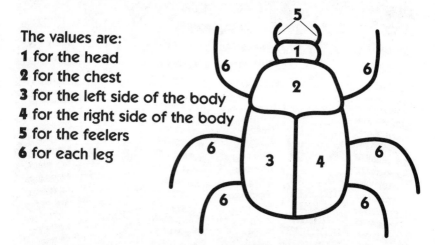

Obviously you can't draw the feelers until you have
drawn the head, or the legs until the part of the body
they join has been completed, but otherwise the order
in which you draw your scarab doesn't matter very much.
The first player to complete a scarab wins the game.

CATS' CRADLE

How many models of the cat goddess Bast can you spot hiding in the picture?

WHAT DID BAST THE CAT GODDESS STRIVE FOR?

PURRFECTION!

AT THE OASIS

In the New Kingdom the date palm was an important plant, providing fruit and shade. It was also believed to provide food for the dead. The ancient Egyptians grew a number of trees and other plants in gardens and at oases. All the words listed below connected with deserts and oases can be traced out in the date-palm-shaped grid opposite. They may read across, up, down or diagonally, either forwards or backwards, but they are all in straight lines. Letters may be used more than once, though not all the letters are necessarily used.

Use a pencil and a ruler to help you find them.

ACACIA

ARID

BARREN

CULTIVATE

DATE PALM (2 lines)

DESERT

DOUM PALM (2 lines)

DROUGHT

DUNES

DUST

FIG TREE (2 lines)

FISHPOOL

HEAT

GARDEN

LEMON TREE (2 lines)

LILIES

MIMOSA

OASIS

PERSEA TREE (2 lines)

REEDS

SAND

STONY

SUN

TAMARISK

VINES

WASTELAND

WILLOW

WIND

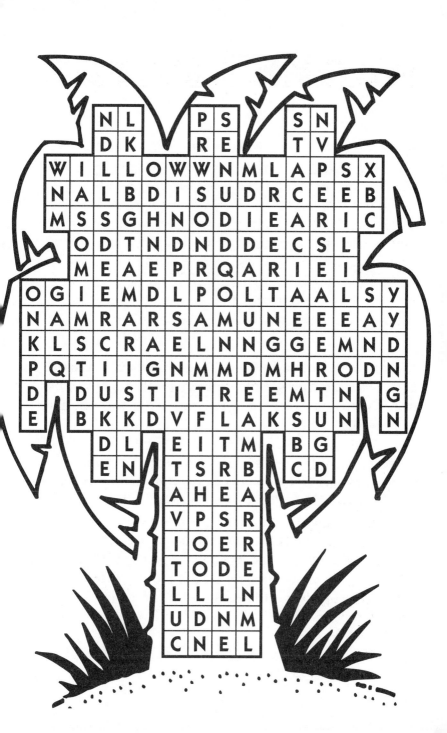

MARKET PLACE

Mouth of Nile

Alexandria

•Heliopolis
•CAIRO

Memphis •

Ancient Egypt traded with other countries in the Middle East. She exported grain and linen, and bought copper from Cyprus, timber from Syria, and cattle and ebony from Nubia.

Three merchants, A, B and C, who live in Memphis, Heliopolis and Cairo, sail boats painted brown, black and white on the River Nile. A, whose boat isn't white, takes grain to Alexandria and returns with a cargo from Syria. B, who lives in Memphis, takes linen to the mouth of the Nile and returns with a cargo from Cyprus. C, whose boat is brown and who lives nearest the mouth of the Nile, takes grain up-river and returns with two other commodities.

Where does each merchant live, what colour is his boat and what cargo does it return with?

MIX AND MATCH

All the words and pictures below are connected with producing food, and each is part of a pair. Can you match the two halves of each pair?

HONEY

CHEESE

BREAD

EGG

WINE

DATES

MILK

PORK

WORD SNAKE

Solve the clues below and enter the answers in the grid, snaking round from left to right, right to left, and back again, from the serpent's head to its tail. All the answers are creatures that lived wild in Egypt at the time of the ancient Egyptians.

1   A kind of deer – its name begins with an insect and ends with a word meaning to run away to get married *(8)*
2   A very large animal that lives in rivers – its name means 'river horse' *(12)*
3   A big cat known as 'the king of beasts' *(4)*
4   Another river creature - this one lies under water with its big jaws waiting to snap at its prey *(9)*
5   A wild dog-like animal that hunts in packs – its name sounds like someone saying hello to a girl or woman *(5)*
6   Another kind of deer – its name begins with the first three letters of the nickname of a famous footballer *(7)*
7   A large bird which sounds like a lifting device on a building site *(5)*
8   A poisonous snake – its first word is something there's a lot of in the desert; its second is a word meaning 'venomous serpent' *(4, 5)*
9   Small creature with claws like a lobster and a deadly sting in its tail *(8)*
10 The kind of snake seen on the headdresses of some of the ancient Egyptians *(5)*
11 A large deer with straight horns – an anagram of 'Roy X' *(4)*

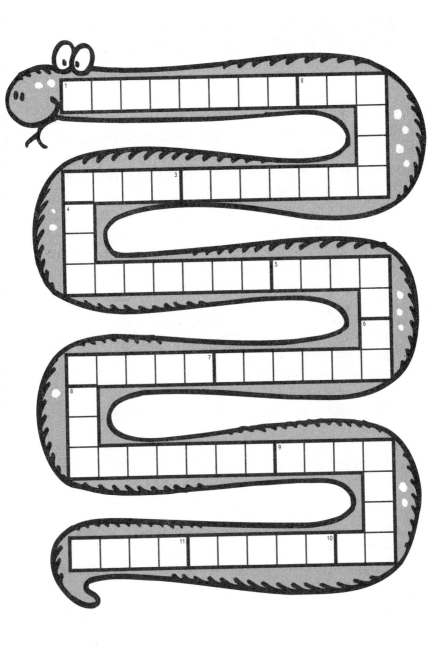

MEMORY TEST

The picture on the right is a copy of a painting on the tomb of Sennedjem, one of the builders of the tombs in the Valley of the Kings. On the left are Sennedjem and his wife; on the right is a shrine depicting Osiris (top left), Horus (below left) and other gods of the Underworld. Look at the picture carefully for one whole minute (time yourself with a watch), then cover it up with a sheet of paper and see how many of the questions below you can answer. Don't cheat!

1 How many figures are standing up?
2 Which figure has a disc on his/her head?
3 Which figure has a flower on his/her head?
4 Who is holding a flower?
5 How many figures have beards?
6 Which god has a falcon's head?
7 How many lines of hieroglyphs are there between the gods?
8 What kind of shoes are Sennedjem and his wife wearing?
9 What kind of clothes is Sennedjem wearing?
10 How many of the figures have raised hands?

HOW'S YOUR BROTHER THESE DAYS? I'D HEARD HE WAS A BIT MISERABLE.

YES, HE'S TOTALLY WRAPPED UP IN HIMSELF!

29

WHICH GOD?

Below are pictures of three ancient Egyptian gods: Anubis, the jackal, Sekhmet, the lioness and Khnum, the ram. On the opposite page are a number of pieces. If they are put together properly, which god will they make up?

ANUBIS SEKHMET KHNUM

CRYPTIC CROSSWORD

Across

1 Charles, initially, can hurt, but it all makes an amulet *(5)*

4 Snake that's good at maths? *(5)*

7 Pot to hold ashes sounds like getting a wage *(3)*

9 The ancient Egyptians made theirs from soot and papyrus juice – and wrote with it *(3)*

10 Sunrise begins it *(3)*

11 Direction, a compass point between North and North-East *(1,1,1)*

12 Bread is baked in it *(4)*

13 Stingers that produce honey *(4)*

14 Main part of a mummy – and of a daddy? *(4)*

17 Food – or food taken *(4)*

20 Not well *(3)*

21 E.g. Osiris *(3)*

23 Tree that sounds like the opposite of ME *(3)*

24 . . . . and sheep that does, too! *(3)*

25 Kingdom *(5)*

26 It makes up the River Nile – and your tea! *(5)*

Down

1 Ancient country's modern capital *(5)*

2 Leg joint the Egyptians sometimes wore jewels around *(5)*

3 Brought by the river, it enabled crops to be grown *(3)*

4 If you don't mind which one you have, you might say you'll have - - - *(3)*

5 People did this at banquets to entertain the guests *(5)*

6 Papyrus is one – sounds as if magazines might be another *(5)*

8 We get a lot of this in Britain – but Egypt has very little *(4)*

14 Wild rose *(5)*

15 The part of the Nile near the Mediterranean Sea *(5)*

16 The - - - - of the Nile is towards the Mediterranean *(4)*

18 The country this book is all about *(5)*

19 The part of 18 Down that is near 15 Down is called this *(5)*

21 Jewel *(3)*

22 Morning moisture that's owing? *(3)*

This puzzle is a bit more difficult than the earlier one. Although some clues are straightforward, you must also pit your wits against cryptic clues, that is, those with hidden meanings, as in a proper grown-up crossword.

WHO DOES A MUMMY TAKE TO THE CINEMA?

ANY OLD PAL HE CAN DIG UP!

CLEVER CALCULATIONS

The ancient Egyptians also had hieroglyphs representing numbers. Seven signs represented values in multiples of ten:

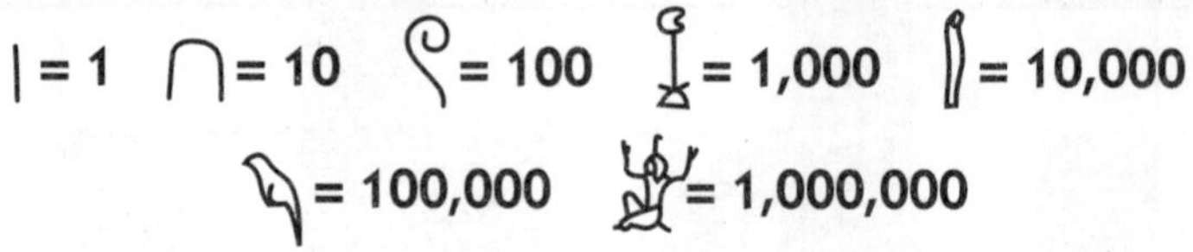

| = 1   ∩ = 10   ℃ = 100   ⚊ = 1,000   ⎰ = 10,000

⎞ = 100,000   𓁨 = 1,000,000

When written down to form a single number, higher values are written in front of lower ones, and multiples of each are shown by repeating the sign.

For example,

4 = | | | |

15 = ∩ | | | | |

260 = ℃℃ ∩∩∩
         ∩∩∩

3789 = ⚊⚊⚊ ℃℃℃℃℃℃℃ ∩∩∩∩
                              ∩∩∩∩ | | | | | | | | |

It takes up a lot of space, doesn't it, but it's really quite simple.

Using this number system, see if you can work out what the following sums represent.

1

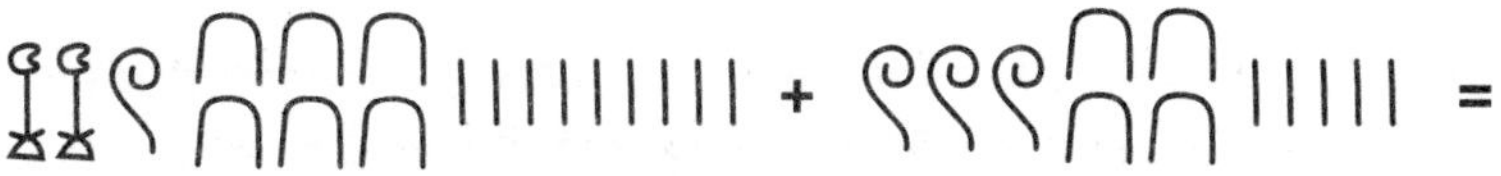

𓀀𓀀 𓂀 ∩∩∩ / ∩∩∩ | | | | | | | | | + ゟゟゟ ∩∩ | | | | | =

2

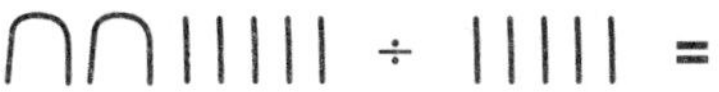

∩∩ | | | | | ÷ | | | | | =

3

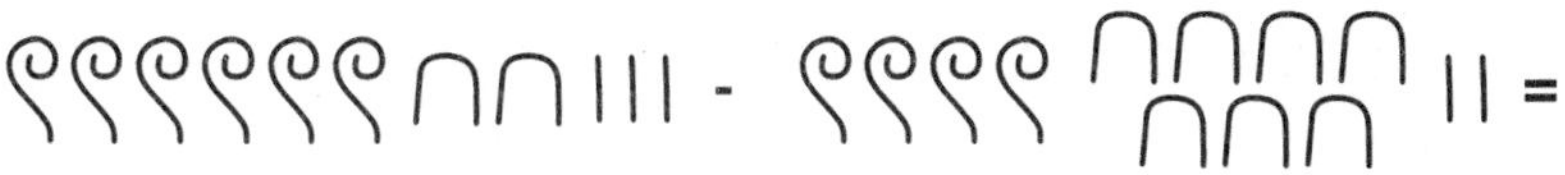

ゟゟゟゟゟゟ ∩∩ | | | - ゟゟゟゟ ∩∩∩∩ / ∩∩∩ | | =

4

∩ | | | | | | × | | | | | =

5

𓀀 ゟゟゟゟゟゟゟゟ ⫷⫷⫷⫷ 𓀀𓀀𓀀 ゟゟ ∩∩∩ / ∩∩ | | | | | | |

+

𓀀 ゟゟゟゟゟゟゟゟ ⫷⫷ 𓀀 ゟゟゟゟゟ ∩∩∩ / ∩∩∩ | | | =

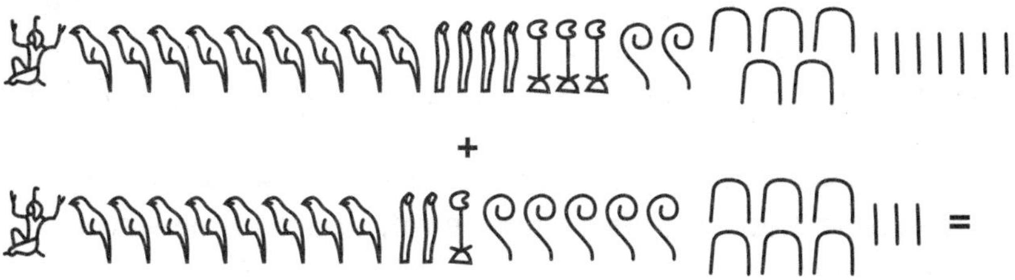

ALL IN A DAY'S WORK

Ancient Egypt had many skilled craftsmen – carpenters, metal-workers, glass-makers, jewellers, tanners, makers of pottery and weavers of cloth. The answers to this puzzle are all connected with their work. Solve the clues and write the answers in the grid. The arrowed column will then spell out two Egyptian words meaning 'workers in stone and wood' and 'workers with clay'.

1. See 2.
2. and 1. Revolving disc clay is put on to shape it into a vessel (7, 5)
3. Metal-working process in which metal is extracted from ore (similar to the word used for an ice-cream when it gets warm!) (8)
4. Pot in which metals are heated to make them molten (8)
5. Hard stone used by prehistoric Egyptians as a blade (5)
6. Kind of soil used to make pottery (4)
7. Cutting implement made from rock and used to prepare bodies for embalming (5, 5)
8. In the New Kingdom these were used to blow air into the fire for heating metal (7)
9. Wooden peg on which flax fibres were wound for weaving (7)
10. When you wet (6) for pottery-making you are said to do this to it (the word also means a small pool of rainwater on the ground) (6)

THROUGH A MIRROR

Below is a picture of the Sphinx, and around it are four pictures which show its mirror image. But only one of them shows the correct mirror image. Which picture is it?

WHAT DO MUMMIES DO AT 11 O'CLOCK EACH MORNING?

TAKE A COFFIN BREAK!

HOW MANY DIFFERENCES...

... can you spot between these two pictures of people using a shaduf to raise water?

PLAY THE GAME

Board games were very popular in ancient Egypt, and the most popular was *senet*, played on a rectangular board divided into three rows of ten squares each.

Some of the boards which have been found have little drawers underneath for the counters, which looked a bit like chessmen. Two players had seven men each, and the object of the game was to get all your men off the board before your opponent did.

The ancient Egyptians didn't have dice, so they fixed how far they could move their men by throwing little sticks, which were rounded on one side and flat on the other. The number of sticks that fell flat sides uppermost was the number of squares they could move in that go.

You can make your own game of *senet* to play with a friend. You will need a sheet of paper, a pen or pencil, a ruler, a die and shaker and some counters. You may find it easier to use just five counters each at first, so you'll need five of two different colours, or you could use small coins.

If you want to be really authentic you could make your own throwing sticks from old lollipop sticks. Save six, and paint an animal's head on one side of each. Count the number of head sides that land uppermost when you throw them to determine how far you can move your counters.

First draw your 'board' on a sheet of paper. Draw a rectangle with sides of 25 cm x 7.5 cm (about 10 x 3 inches), and mark it off into 2.5 cm (1 inch) sections. Join these with lines to make 30 squares.

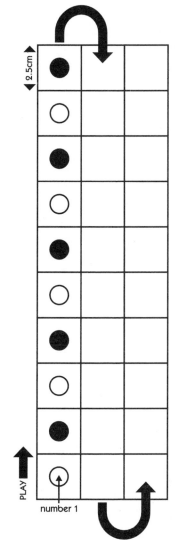

2.5cm

PLAY

number 1

Place the counters alternately along one side of the board. The aim is for each player to move their counters along the board in a zig-zag, first one way, then the other, then to the right again and off the board. Start with counter number 1, your counter furthest to the left. Shake the die or cast the sticks to see how far you can move it. If you land on a square occupied by one of your own counters stay there, but if you land on a square occupied by one of your opponent's counters, you must return to the beginning again. Your opponent then has a turn, starting with his or her counter furthest to the left. Continue in this way, and when your first counter has travelled round the board and off the other end, start again with the second counter, and so on until all your counters are off the board. Whoever manages to do this first wins the game.

HOW MANY PHARAOHS?

How many times can you spot the word PHARAOH in the grid below? The words may run across, up, down or diagonally, either forwards or backwards, but they are all in straight lines.

P	H	A	R	O	A	H	A	R	A	H	P
H	H	O	A	R	A	H	P	P	P	P	P
A	O	A	A	H	P	O	H	H	H	H	A
R	A	A	R	O	H	A	A	A	A	A	R
A	R	R	R	A	A	R	R	R	R	R	H
O	A	H	A	A	O	A	A	A	A	A	O
H	P	O	H	O	H	H	O	O	O	O	A
H	O	A	R	A	H	P	H	H	H	H	R
P	H	R	A	H	O	A	R	A	H	P	A
H	O	A	R	A	H	P	H	A	R	O	H
O	P	H	A	R	H	O	A	R	A	H	P
A	H	P	H	A	R	A	O	H	O	A	R

HOW MANY PYRAMIDS ...

... are there in this picture?

PICTURE MESSAGE

Can you read what the pictures on this page spell out?
The letters and the plus or minus signs show what must
be added or subtracted from the word suggested by the
picture to give the word of the message.

WHAT'S WRONG?

Here's a copy of a Theban painting, found on a wooden chest in Tutankhamun's tomb. Can you spot all the things that are wrong with it?

SCRAMBLED SENTENCES

The words of these sentences have been printed in the wrong order. Can you make sense out of them?

1   1922 Carter of the Tutankhamun discovered Howard 26 on November tomb.

2   Artists made the finds early they took record before Egyptologists photography with them to the days of.

3   At the Step King about Djoser was built of Saqqara 2,650 BC Imhotep by architect his chief Pyramid.

4   The meaning of the 1820s discovered in Egyptian hieroglyphs of an inscribed the Jean François Champollion Rosetta help with the stone called the Stone.

5   Of Menkaura and those of Giza Great King with Khafre stands the Pyramid at Khufu.

6   The Great cathedrals hold St Peter's is St Paul's large enough to the Milan Florence plus those of Westminster Abbey Pyramid and London and of Rome.

7   At Sneferu 'Bent' the angle in the middle Maidum whose sides their King built Pyramid change.

8   'Mummies' believed the ancient Egyptians pre-served a life created for the soul because they had to be a person's body to have after death.

ODD ONE OUT

Which of these depictions of the cartouche of King Djoser's name is the odd one out, and why?

THE RIGHT PLACE

Each of the words listed below can be fitted into a place in the grid opposite. You have to find out where they all go. Five letters have been given to help you start.

3 letters
TOD

4 letters
EDFU
LYRE
SETH

5 letters
KAMAK
KHNUM

6 letters
KARNAK
NATRON

7 letters
DYNASTY
PAPYRUS
PTOLEMY
SAQQARA
SNEFERU

8 letters
KHEPHREN
THUTMOSE

10 letters
HATSHEPSUT

11 letters
SARCOPHAGUS

HOW DOES A MUMMY BEGIN A LETTER?

TOMB IT MAY CONCERN...

THE REAL KING

If a real king wore gold, had a long, narrow plaited beard with the end sticking forwards, wore an ornate wig, a headdress with a cobra on the front, a large ornamental collar, a pleated kilt and sandals, which of the kings pictured below is the real one?

THE MUMMY'S CURSE

If you study this creepy picture carefully you will discover that three of the squares into which the picture has been divided are identical. Which three squares are they?

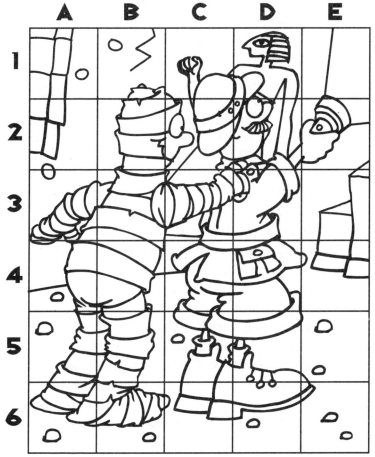

CLUELESS

This is a crossword puzzle with a difference, for it has no clues! Instead, the words missing from the paragraph below form the answers which must be fitted into the grid opposite. The information in brackets tells you where they should go, and the story should give enough hints to form the 'clues'. Are you up to the challenge?

Fill in the easy answers first: their letters will help you solve the more difficult ones.

In the - - - - (2 Down, 3 letters) **Kingdom, which covers dynasties 18-20 and existed about 3,000** - - - - (4 Down, 5 letters) **ago,** - - - - (14 Across, 5 letters) **was ruled by a** - - - - (23 Across, 6 letters) **pharaoh called Queen Hatshepsut. She** - - - - (22 Across, 5 letters) **in partnership with her stepson, who** - - - - (5 Across, 3 letters) **later to become** - - - - (6 Down, 4 letters). - - - - (11 Across, 3 letters) **name was Thutmose III.** - - - - (1 Down, 8 letters) **were usually male, and perhaps to avoid** - - - - (18 Down, 7 letters) **and controversy, Queen** - - - - (17 Across, 10 letters) **is often** - - - - (9 Across, 5 letters) **in pictures and statues dressed in the** - - - - (12 Down, 5 letters) **and fashion of a king and wearing a false** - - - - (16 Down, 5 letters) **on her chin. The Queen's beautiful** - - - - (15 Down, 6 letters)**, where the priests served the gods, is built of** - - - - (19 Down, 5 letters) **surrounded by** - - - - (4 Across, 6 letters) **sand, with cliffs behind it. This** - - - - (21 Across, 5 letters) **building provides a spectacular**

setting for Verdi's - - - - (10 Down, 5 letters) *Aida,* **which is
- - - -** (13 Across, 3 letters) **in - - - -** (8 Down, 7 letters)
Egypt. Queen Hatshepsut's - - - - (20 Down, 4 letters) **is in
the - - - -** (3 Across, 6 letters) **of the Kings, and was
discovered by - - - -** (7 Across, 6 letters) **Carter in 1903.**

WHAT DO YOU CALL A
MUMMY WHO EATS
TREACLE SANDWICHES?

A GUMMY
MUMMY!

53

FISH AND SHIPS

How many differences can you spot between these two pictures of people fishing in the Nile?

FIELD DAY

These men are leading their cattle out to pasture but the lead ropes have got tangled up. Which man is leading which animal?

RIDDLE OF THE SANDS

Can you solve this brain-teasing riddle?

My first is in Thebes, but never in Nile,
My second's the shape your mouth makes with a smile.
My third is in Thutmose, trade and translation,
My fourth is in Nubia, national and nation.
My fifth's like a chicken with its H dropped,
My sixth's a girl's name with its last letters chopped.
My seventh is found in both Hathor and Horus,
My eighth is in harpist but never in chorus.
My ninth starts Menkaura, of pyramid fame,
My tenth ends Sneferu, well-known for the same.
My last's found in Karnak, whose temples are tall,
My whole's the most famous young king of them all!

WHAT DO YOU CALL A MUMMY WITH A PAPER BAG ON HIS HEAD?

RUSSELL!

EYE, EYE!

Below is a drawing of an amulet depicting the hieroglyph of the sacred eye of Horus. Which of the negatives of the picture surrounding it is the correct one?

LOTS OF LOTUS

If a lotus flower looks like this 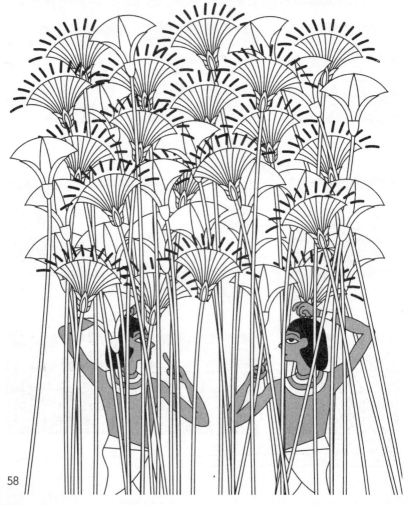, and a papyrus stalk looks like this how many lotus flowers and how many papyrus stalks can you spot in the picture?

ANSWERS

Page 6 Monumental

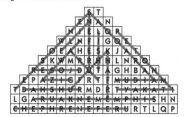

Page 8 Building Costs
1. 150,000 sq m.
2. 575,000 of each.
3. 54.5 **khars** of wheat;
    20 **khars** of barley.

Page 9 Birds of a Feather
Pictures no. 2 and 3 are exactly alike.

Page 10 Reading and Writing
1. Rat.   4. Lark.
2. Trap.   5. Port.
3. Plait.

Page 12 It's the Best!
1. Nile.
2. Aswan.
3. Abu Simbel.
4. Ramses.
5. Memphis.
6. Isis.
7. Bast.
8. Osiris.
9. Horus.
10. Mummy.

Page 13
Find the Tomb

Page 14 Quick Quiz
1. c) Giza.
2. b) A body with its organs removed.
3. a) 18.
4. a) The head of a man and the body
    of a lion.
5. c) The stem of a reed.
6. b) A kind of make-up.
7. a) Around 2,500 BC.
8. c) A king of Egypt.
9. a) Every year.
10. c) Hieroglyphs.

Page 15 In the House

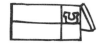

appears in every frame except no. 1.

Page 16
Crack the Crossword

Page 18 **Egyptian Louts**
1. Pharaoh.
2. Abu Simbel.
3. Priestess.
4. Cleopatra.
5. Imhotep.
6. Hatshepsut.
7. Papyrus.
8. Anubis.

Page 19
How Many Differences . .?

Page 21 **Cats' Cradle**
There are 8 models of Bast in the picture.

Page 22 **At the Oasis**

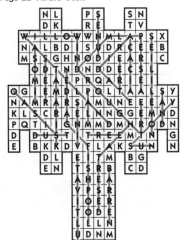

Page 24 **Market Place**
Merchant A lives in Cairo, sails a black boat and brings back timber from Syria.
Merchant B lives in Memphis, sails a white boat and brings back copper from Cyprus.
Merchant C lives in Heliopolis, sails a brown boat and brings back ebony and cattle from Nubia.

Page 25 **Mix and Match**
Bee - honey; milk - cow or goat; egg - goose; bread - wheat; wine - grapes; dates - date palm; pork - pig; cheese - cow or goat.

Page 26 **Word Snake**

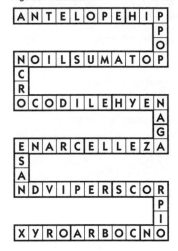

Page 28 **Memory Test**
1. Two.
2. The god Horus (second from right in bottom corner).
3. Sennedjem's wife (lady on the left).
4. Sennedjem's wife.
5. Three.
6. Horus (second from right in bottom corner).
7. Three.
8. They aren't wearing shoes.
9. A kilt tied round his waist.
10. Two - Sennedjem and his wife.

Page 30 **Which God?**
Khnum.

C	H	A	R	M		A	D	D	E	R
A		N		U	R	N		A		E
I	N	K		D	A	Y		N	E	E
R		L			I			C		D
O	V	E	N			N		B	E	E	S
B	O	D	Y		F		M	E	A	L
R		E			L		G		O
I	L	L		G	O	D		Y	E	W
A		T		E	W	E		P		E
R	E	A	L	M		W	A	T	E	R

Page 34 **Clever Calculations**

1. 2,514.
2. 5.
3. 151.
4. 80.
5. 3,764,820.

Page 36 **All in a Day's Work**

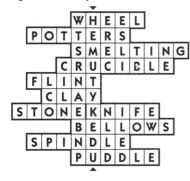

The arrowed column spells out *hemuty*, which means 'workers in stone and wood', and *kedu*, 'workers with clay'.

Page 38 **Through a Mirror**
Picture no. 4.
(1 has no ear, 2 has no lines on neck and 3 has its ear reversed.)

Page 39 **How Many Differences. . . ?**

Seven differences.

Page 42
How Many Pharaohs?

There are 15 PHARAOHs in the grid.

Page 43 **How Many Pyramids?**
13.

Page 44 **Picture Message**
The message is:
Craftsmen beat gold into thin sheets to decorate objects.

Page 45 What's Wrong?

1. The king is wearing Doc Marten's on his feet.
2. On his belt is a mobile phone.
3. In the background is a modern street sign.
4. The king's headdress is decorated with a mouse instead of a cobra.
5. The queen is wearing a wrist-watch.
6. The king's belt and tab are tartan, not striped.
7. In the background is a toddler in a push-chair.
8. Also in the background two children are playing cricket.
9. On the queen's head are salt and pepper pots.
10. The king is wearing spectacles.

Page 46
Scrambled Sentences

1. Howard Carter discovered the tomb of Tutankhamun on 26 November 1922.
2. Before the days of photography, early Egyptologists took with them artists to record the finds they made.
3. The Step Pyramid of King Djoser at Saqqara was built about 2,650 BC by his chief architect, Imhotep.
4. Jean François Champollion discovered the meaning of the Egyptian hieroglyphs in the 1820s, with the help of an inscribed stone called the Rosetta Stone.
5. At Giza stands the Great Pyramid of King Khufu, with those of Menkaura and Khafre.
6. The Great Pyramid is large enough to hold the cathedrals of St Paul's and Westminster Abbey, London, plus those of Milan, Florence and St Peter's, Rome.
7. King Sneferu built the 'Bent' Pyramid, whose sides change their angle in the middle, at Maidum.
8. The ancient Egyptians created 'mummies' because they believed a person's body had to be preserved for the soul to have a life after death.

Page 47 Odd One Out
Picture no. 7 is the odd one out.

Page 48 The Right Place

Page 50 The Real King
King no. 3 is the real king.

Page 51 The Mummy's Curse
Frames 2A, 4E & 6C.